Ho

# How to Backpack Europe on a Budget

# HowExpert with Kacey Andreacola

## Copyright HowExpert™
## www.HowExpert.com

**For more tips related to this topic, visit HowExpert.com/backpackeurope.**

# Recommended Resources

- HowExpert.com – Quick 'How To' Guides on All Topics from A to Z by Everyday Experts.
- HowExpert.com/free – Free HowExpert Email Newsletter.
- HowExpert.com/books – HowExpert Books
- HowExpert.com/courses – HowExpert Courses
- HowExpert.com/membership – HowExpert Membership Site
- HowExpert.com/writers – Write About Your #1 Passion/Knowledge/Expertise & Become a HowExpert Author.
- HowExpert.com/resources – Additional HowExpert Recommended Resources
- YouTube.com/HowExpert – Subscribe to HowExpert YouTube.
- Instagram.com/HowExpert – Follow HowExpert on Instagram.
- Facebook.com/HowExpert – Follow HowExpert on Facebook.

# Table of Contents

# Introduction

If you're interested in backpacking through Europe, this is a great place to start! I was in Europe for four months and spent an average of $50 a day. It took some discipline, but it allowed me to have many different experiences and adventures. Prioritizing and research led to a great trip, wonderful memories and some savings when I got home. Don't let the thought of the expense keep you from fulfilling a dream!

# Chapter 1: Set Your Budget

## 1.1 Money in the Bank

In order to successfully backpack on a budget, you actually need to set a budget. This seems obvious, but if you do not put thought into it now, it will quickly get out of hand once you arrive. Look at how much you have saved for the trip. Find out what the current exchange rate is in each of the countries you intend to travel in. For example, the US dollar might be stronger than the Polish zloty. However, the euro is likely stronger than the dollar. Look at the recent trends and keep the exchange rate in mind.

Another important thing to consider while setting your budget is how you intend to pay for things. You can either pull cash from ATMs, use a credit card, use a debit card or exchange dollars in an airport or other location. Any combination of these is also an option. Keep in mind that different cards have different policies. I used a credit card that did not charge a foreign transaction fee, so I ended up paying only the fee for converting dollars to the necessary currency. Then, I just paid off the credit card each month.

I also used a debit card that does not charge ATM fees. This means that I could use my debit card to get cash in any country for free, again only paying the fee to convert currencies, which was a much smaller percentage. This combination allowed me to have access to cash pretty much anywhere, but also not have to worry about carrying large amounts of cash around with me. I could take more cash out of an ATM as often as I wanted.

## 1.2 Prioritizing

While setting your budget, consider what is important to you. Do you want to stay in nice rooms? Eat good meals? Take guided tours? Buy souvenirs? Prioritize where you want to spend your money. Personally, I wanted to see as much as I could and enjoy good meals. So I was much more willing to stay in hostels and shared rooms. And I ended up not purchasing more than two souvenirs the whole time I was there. However, I saw pretty much everything I wanted to see.

## 1.3 Safety Net

Once you have an idea of how much you're willing to spend and where you want to be spending your money, look at how much you anticipate spending each day. Then, add a safety net to that. Each day will likely average out, as some will cost you more and others will be less expensive. The prices in each country will also vary and it will tend to even out by the end of the trip.

To give you an idea, I spent an average of $50 per day. You also need to calculate in the cost of transportation to the country and possibly transportation within the country. There will be more on transportation later. However, it is important to have an idea of what you can afford to spend each day and try to stick with it throughout the trip.

You will be able to enjoy your trip even more if you are not overly worried about money and your budget. Just know what you want to spend and do your best to stick with it throughout the trip. In the rest of this guide, I will be working off of a presumed budget of $50 a day. However, feel free to adjust to whatever your budget is.

# Chapter 2: Packing

## 2.1 Purchasing a Backpack

In order to have a fun and successful backpacking trip, you'll need to have a good backpack. This is a place where you may need to spend some money, but it will be worth it to have a backpack that works exactly for your situation.

You will definitely want a backpack that is comfortable and that you can wear for long hours. Ideally, you will not need to have your backpack on for a long time, but you should be prepared for that possibility. Also, you want a backpack that is smaller and can fit in the overhead compartment on the plane. Each airline has different regulations, but international airlines usually require carry-on bags to be smaller than airlines in the United States. Using a carry-on for a roundtrip flight will save you at least $100, which leaves you with two extra days of spending!

A good backpack will probably cost between $100 and $200. However, if you know enough ahead of time, consider watching the sales before you purchase one. You will not need to break it in, so it is a purchase that you can put off until close to the end. Then, if it does not go on sale, you will still spend the same amount of money.

## 2.2 Filling the Backpack

Once you have an idea of the backpack you want, consider how you are going to fill it. (Quick note: It may be worth purchasing a backpack and leaving the tags on, just for size consideration, even if it's not the exact bag you want. Then you can return it later.) I took a 30 liter backpack for 4 months, and it was the perfect size. There are some backpacks that can be used as suitcases, but that is just up to personal preference. There is not any financial benefit to either of these styles.

## 2.3 Packing List

While picking a backpack, you can also begin to consider what you plan to pack. The items you take will make a difference in your budget. Again, there may be a cost upfront, but what you pack can save you money when you arrive.

First and foremost, you will want good shoes that go with everything else you plan to take. If your feet hurt and you cannot walk very far, you will have to pay for transportation more often. If you choose not to, you risk being in pain and not getting to fully enjoy the sights.

The next important item to take is a good rain jacket. Again, spend the money on this, as it will allow you to enjoy many different sights and activities, regardless of the weather. Many people do not prepare for this, and instead end up buying plastic ponchos over and over, or spending money on a jacket while in Europe. This can get expensive.

Beyond these two necessities, you will just want to be sure you take clothes that can be washed in the sink and will not get smelly too quickly. Take single use detergent packs with you so you can wash your clothes in the sink as much as possible. This will save you money and also keep you from having to wait in lines to use laundry facilities.

As a quick overview, here's an example list of what you will want to pack:

- 3-5 shirts (both long and short sleeves)
- 3 bottoms (jeans, capris, khaki shorts, skirt, etc.)
- Sweater
- Rain jacket
- Closed toe shoes
- Sandals
- Socks/underwear
- Pajamas (that could possibly double as clothes to swim in)
- Toiletries
- Scarf
- Towel
- Water bottle

Of course, you may also want things like a camera, phone, travel journal, sleeping bag liner, etc. However, this leaves you with a pretty comprehensive list of clothing items that will allow you to be flexible based on the weather and the plan for the day. Toiletries are not any more expensive in Europe than they are in the States, so take what you think you will need and then buy something if you want it later on. You want to be prepared with just enough clothes and not overwhelmed with a bunch of small bottles.

One important thing to note is that you will absolutely want to take a water bottle. Water is not free in most of Europe, so you will definitely save money by filling up your water bottle each morning. If you have to get water twice a day, you're looking at about 4 USD each day, which will add up quickly.

I understand that some people might already be thinking this kind of trip would be too much just because of the packing requirements. Let me reassure you, you *can* pack like this. My parents and in-laws met us at different parts of our trip and all four of them packed in a backpack and traveled like this with us. Don't think this is only for young, crazy people. If this is what you want to do, you will figure out a way to leave the six extra shirts at home. It's worth it.

It is hard to anticipate exactly what you will need, so you may end up leaving things behind as you go. With this in mind, do not take anything that is your favorite! You might ruin it or end up needing to leave it behind. Yes, you might want to look good in all the pictures, but leave your very favorites at home.

# Chapter 3: Traveling to Europe

## 3.1 Time of Year

The prices at most of the tourist-related things in Europe vary depending on the time of year. The summer is the most expensive time to go because it is the most popular and tends to have the best weather over the majority of the continent. However, if you go in the winter, you risk that many sights will be closed or have shortened hours. Also, you will have to pack much differently and winter will require heavier clothes and more layers.

With this in mind, either spring or fall is usually the best time to go. This allows you to pack a bit lighter than the dead of winter would allow for, but also gives you the best chance that the sights you want to go to are actually open. I went July through November and didn't encounter anything that was closed because of the season. I also did not encounter super cold weather, which was just generally more pleasant.

August is usually the busiest month in many cities, so you will save money and time waiting in lines if you are in some of the smaller cities or towns that you want to visit during August. Most of the smaller towns are usually more expensive anyway, so you are paying what you would pay any time of year, rather than paying an inflated price in the big cities because it is tourist season.

Ultimately, you have to do what works in your schedule. However, if you have the flexibility, you will save money depending on when you travel and where you are during the busy season.

## 3.2 Countries

Part of setting your budget includes planning through what you want to see. It is incredibly important to get an idea of which countries you absolutely do not want to miss. Spend some time doing research and figuring out what is most interesting and appealing to you. Ask people who have been to Europe what they liked and what they would not necessarily recommend. Even if they went on a business trip or a cruise, you can learn something from them about how you want to plan your trip.

Keep in mind that even though a country is in Europe, it is not necessarily part of the European Union. This means that there are going to be different currencies, especially if you go into the Scandinavian countries or into Eastern Europe. Try to get a basic handle on the exchange rate of each country you plan to visit. If you do not have enough knowledge to do a quick calculation of the cost in USD, you risk overspending out of confusion. It is a good idea to look up the exchange rate before you enter a country to make sure you are on the right track.

# 3.3 Plane Tickets

Once you have an idea of where you want to go, start looking at plane tickets. It is very possible that splitting up the ticket will save you money. For example, you could fly a more regional airline to get to a major airport and then fly to Europe with an international airline. This will require a bit more work to make all the travel arrangements, but it could save you a lot of money. This also gives you the option of using points you may have accrued that would otherwise not be available for use with an international airline. You could potentially fly in the States for free and only need to pay for one direct flight into Europe. Alternatively, if you live near a major airport that does international flights to Europe, you only need to worry about one flight.

Obviously, flying coach is going to be cheaper. In addition to this, being flexible with your travel time will allow you to get a better rate. If you use Google Flights to look up costs, it has an option for flexible dates. Also, you will want to fly a budget airline if at all possible. Because it is guaranteed to be a long flight, almost all airlines will have some sort of food available for purchase when you book the ticket. Some airlines will bundle things together, including a checked bag, a meal and the option to choose your seat.

I was travelling with my husband, so we chose to spend the extra $50 to guarantee a seat together and get the meal. It did seem a bit expensive but, for us, it was money well spent. Throughout your trip your spending will be based on your priorities, so it will likely look different from mine. However, the main thing is to be conscious of the choices you are making; this will help you keep to your budget and still enjoy as much as possible.

If your travel plans are flexible, consider flying into the city that is the cheapest. For example, most of the UK tends to be pretty expensive. You may want to fly in to somewhere in the EU. You may also find that flights are cheaper if you go into one of the Scandinavian countries. Prices will vary depending on the day of the week you are flying, the time of day and the season. You will need to pick based on what works best for your plan.

## 3.4 Route

While deciding on where to fly in, it may be helpful to make a basic route. This does not mean that you have to follow it exactly once you arrive, but you may want an idea of which country you intend to fly into and where you would like to end your trip. It is almost always going to be better to fly out of a different city than you flew into, especially if you are planning to see more than one country.

There are a number of budget airlines that offer incredibly cheap flights (think $30-$75) that could get you back to your entrance point, but it would be more convenient to simply fly out of where you end your trip. Also, depending on how long you plan to stay, you may want to wait until sometime in the middle of your trip to book the flight home.

In order to illustrate this idea, I will tell you the specifics of how my husband and I did it. We knew we wanted to go as far north as Norway and then intended to see everything on the mainland that was south and west of that. We looked at tickets on the peripherals of the area we wanted to see, as well as considered a basic route that would allow us to see parts of each of those countries.

Ultimately, based on the tickets available and the countries we had listed, we chose to fly into Norway. The tickets were reasonable and this would allow us to move south, never needing to retrace our route back into the Scandinavian countries. Then, because we knew we would be there for a while, we waited until the second month before we bought our tickets home. By that time, we had an idea of how things worked and the pace we were moving at. We chose to fly out of Italy, as we had plans to meet some family there the last couple weeks of our trip. We did not have quite as much flexibility when choosing where to fly out. However, when you consider the cost of getting to a different airport, the difference between the cheaper ticket and the extra travelling tends to even out.

In all of these decisions, it is really necessary to consider where you want to go and how long you want to spend in Europe. These choices will help you set parameters and allow you to pick the most cost-effective route, as well as the best flight options.

# Chapter 4: Travelling in Europe

## 4.1 Eurail Pass vs Single Tickets

Once you arrive in Europe, you have many options to choose from regarding how you're going to get around, whether between cities or once you've arrived in a city. There are multiples modes of transportation that can be used for almost any trip. Your choice will depend on the length of the trip, your flexibility on the time, your bag and the cost.

One major thing to consider is the train system. Trains are frequently used as a way to get between cities. Trains are often the most convenient way and allow for quite a bit of flexibility. With that in mind, you will want to consider the possibility of a Eurail pass.

When you have a Eurail pass, it counts as your ticket in Western Europe, as well as a few places in Eastern Europe. The pass is not valid anywhere in the United Kingdom. However it is valid in Northern Ireland, as they are part of the European Union. You can go the Eurail website to find updated information regarding the price of each pass, as well as any rules or exceptions that apply.

There are multiple types of passes. One option is a pass that allows for unlimited rides during a continuous amount of time. Another is a pass that gives you a limited amount of travel days in a set amount of time. Some passes require that you travel only within a certain number of bordering countries. There are a number of options, but the Eurail website has trip-planning help that will allow you to make the best decision for you, especially taking into account the length of your trip and the number of countries you want to see.

If you have a Eurail pass, you will likely still be required to make a reservation for most high-speed train rides. This average cost is anywhere from €6-€20. There is an option to take some of the slower trains that make more stops, but it is usually worth it to pay the reservation fee so that you do not end up spending most of your trip on a train. The trains can be fun, but that is probably not the main reason you are backpacking through Europe.

While reservations may seem expensive in addition to buying the actual pass, it is definitely a money-saver if you intend to travel to quite a few cities. It is also worth it if you have the pass that only allows for a certain number of travel days, as you can quickly cover quite a bit of distance in just one day. If you do not make reservations on high-speed trains, you risk needing to use more travel days for the same distance, therefore not making the best use of your Eurail pass. The pass can also be used to make reservations on overnight trains. If you travel overnight, you do not use any time during the day that you could be sightseeing, and you also do not have to pay for lodging that night. Your reservation on an overnight train is likely the same amount or less compared to what you would pay for a bed – and a bed does not allow you to make ground on your travel plans. This is a major benefit!

When you purchase your Eurail pass, be sure to go through their website and not anything else. They do not offer a full discount, but if your plans change and you have to cancel before you leave, you can get the majority of your money back. Their website has promotions that include extra travel days for free. The pass also has discounts attached to it, such as on ferry rides. It is definitely safer to purchase your pass directly from the Eurail site, as you can be sure there will not be any hidden fees or surprises.

If you plan to remain in one country and really see the whole country, it *might* be worth paying for tickets individually. However, the Eurail pass is designed for non-European travelers so that they can save money and experience Europe by train. It is hard to imagine a scenario where the Eurail pass is not the best option while backpacking Europe. Most likely, you just need to figure out which of the passes will be optimal for you and your trip.

# 4.2 Other Long-Distance Travel Options

Using long-distance buses is another way to get between cities. If you do not purchase a Eurail pass, this is an option. However, it is always slower and there are usually not as many departure time options.

A bus is a good way to get between mainland Europe and the United Kingdom. This is a particularly good way to go if you take an overnight bus. It is cheaper than the Eurostar (AKA chunnel) and you will not have to pay for lodging that evening. However, while you are in a Eurail zone, it is likely the best deal and best use of your time to use the pass.

Flying is a third option that is also very helpful for transportation between the European Union and the United Kingdom, or if you plan to go a long distance without stopping. There are flights between major cities in Europe that range from $35-$100. These are usually with budget airlines that will charge you for everything and spend the majority of the flight time trying to sell you things. However, if your bag fits within the allowed limits and you have enough self-control to avoid purchasing things from them, this is an incredibly cheap and quick way to cover a lot of ground in a very short amount of time.

One thing to note about the flights is that they often leave from somewhat obscure airports. If this is the case, weigh the cost of getting to the airport plus the actual flight. If you need to take a charter bus to get to the airport or pay a taxi, it will get very expensive very quickly. However, this does not mean that it is not the best option. Even if the bus ride to the airport is the same price as the flight, you may only be spending $70 to get a long distance in a very short amount of time.

Ferries are one other way you can get between places. They are oftentimes discounted with the Eurail pass, but tickets can be purchased separately. This is a very unique way to see the coast and get a different perspective on the place you are visiting. However, your decision to ride a ferry will be heavily based on the time and price. This can vary quite a bit between countries.

Once you arrive in a city, there are numerous ways you can get around. Before you leave for your next city, it is helpful to look up some of the main information about the transportation in the city. You want to be sure that you are not getting scammed out of any money and that you are generally picking a reliable and cheap option.

Most of the bigger cities have some kind of local subway or rail system. While it is possible to purchase passes or cards for a certain number of rides, you will likely just want to purchase individual rides, especially if you do not have every single part of your day planned. These are usually pretty reasonably priced and almost always have stops within walking distance of the major tourist destinations. Some are priced based on distance, while others are just a flat rate. Also, if you get the Eurail pass, ask at the information desk if the pass will count as your ticket. In some cities, like Paris, your pass will not help you on the subway, but it will get you onto the train that goes out to Versailles. There is no harm in asking and saving a few euros here and there.

Another transportation option is the bus system. The buses tend to be just a bit cheaper than the trains, although more difficult to navigate, especially if you are not using cell service. Most cities have multiple routes that will take you to the tourist destinations.

They may even get you closer than the subway or rail system. Again, it depends on how confident you are in navigating your way through the city.

Taxis are numerous in most big cities, but almost never the cheapest option. They are tolerable if you have no other choice or are in a public transportation dead-zone, but generally not a good way to save money. If you think you may use taxis, you will definitely want to look up what the reliable and public taxi service is in the city.

Depending on the city you are in, water taxis are a quick and cheap way to get around. For example, Venice is not a very big city. However, there is a limited amount of routes available because of the location of the main bridges. It may be a short distance if you could walk in a straight line, but you could also end up going out of your way quite a bit to get to a destination. In this case, the water taxi is probably a good choice, even if it seems like you could and should walk.

Renting a bicycle or going on a bike tour are both great ways to get you around the city, while also enjoying the things in the city. Bike tours are usually pretty reasonable and you may be able to get a discount code or coupon by going to a visitor's center. If you rent a bike, you can go anywhere you want, lock it up and check something out. This allows you to cover more ground than walking, but also to get a more intimate feel for the city. Bike tours are a great way to see a lot of places pretty quickly. If you do not have long to spend in a city, this will give you a chance to have a more personal tour than a bus tour. Many

European cities are biker friendly, but be sure to pay attention to the laws and which side of the road you are supposed to cycle on.

One of my absolute favorite parts of my trip was a Sound of Music bike tour in Salzburg, Austria. I got a lot of information about a musical that I love, while getting to see places that the movie was filmed. I also got out to a few different parts surrounding the town that I would have otherwise not seen by foot and were inaccessible via public transportation.

An option that could be helpful but will cost you extra is to rent a car. If you're planning to stay in and around a major city, this is definitely not necessary and would likely make your whole experience more stressful. However, if you want to see some of the places that are more rural or difficult to access via public transportation, this is possibly a good way to go. It is important that you compare the full price of the trip while considering if you want to rent a car. For example, if you need to take a train and then a long taxi ride, it might be worth renting a car. However, you also need to check if there is a place to park the car and how much it might cost you to park overnight or for an extended amount of time. Renting a car is not a sure way to save money, but it could allow you to see some less-visited places.

Similar to renting a car, you can use a ride-sharing option. You can usually find someone headed in the same direction as you. This gives you the benefit of being able to reach some more rural places without having to rent a car for yourself and consider things like insurance and parking.

There are a number of other ways to get around cities, including boat tours, Segway tours, bus tours and more. If you are in a city with a unique mode of transportation, try it out! This does not mean you have to rely on it the whole time you are there, but it can be fun to see something different and it is usually not very expensive. For example, you could ride the antique tram system in Portugal, a gondola in Venice and an aerial tram in Chamonix. Some of these will be tourist experiences, but that does not mean that they will not help you get from Point A to Point B. If you are getting to sightsee and move about, that is a pretty good deal.

## 4.3 Using Your Legs

The final way to travel within a city is to use your walking legs! This goes back to purchasing good shoes and breaking them in, as well as making sure your backpack is reasonable in size and weight. In a lot of cities, once you arrive in a particular area, you are no more than a mile or two from many tourist destinations. You will get to see a bit more and save your cash if you are willing to walk. This is also a good way to discover places that you may have otherwise just gone right by, including restaurants, shops and local hangouts. If you are not going more than a mile, walking can even be faster than taking public transportation. There is a lot of value in taking in a city by foot.

# Chapter 5: Lodging in Europe

## 5. 1 Hostels, Hotels, Airbnb and More

Depending on your personality, the places that you stay can really affect your trip and your general attitude about your trip. Even if you are not too picky, most people enjoy their time more if they are well-rested and not worried about leaving their few belongings behind. There are a few things to consider about how you want to travel that will make a difference in where you choose to sleep. Also note, when my parents and in-laws met us, they made use of the variety of lodging options. It is okay to modify these preferences to your comfort level, but don't think that your age should stop you from backpacking versus taking a trip planned by a travel company.

Making your own food can save you money (more on that later), so you might want to stay in a place with a kitchen or at least some basic kitchen appliances. You might also want to consider a place that has breakfast included. You will want to stay somewhere that is conveniently located near public transportation. Depending on the length of your stay, you will want some kind of secure luggage room or lockers so that you can confidently leave your backpack behind while you explore for the day. If you do not plan to carry your own sheets and pillows, you will want a place that either includes those in the rate or has them available to rent. You may occasionally want to stay in a hostel with laundry facilities.

You should do all of your booking online, if at all possible. This will allow you to lock in a rate and ensure that a bed/room is available. Even if you do not book until one or two days out, you should still do it online. If you do not, you risk showing up somewhere with no vacancy and being forced to either walk or pay for some sort of transportation to get you to another possible accommodation.

Once you have an idea of the kind of place you are looking for and the general location you want to be in, you need to decide what type of accommodation will fit best. Generally speaking, hostels are going to be your cheapest option. You will likely never find a hotel that has a better price than a hostel. However, there are a few hidden fees or additional costs that you could incur by staying at a hostel.

Again, the total price of your stay at some hostels will increase if you are required to rent the linens. There is no uniformity in what the hostels offer. Some will offer bed linens and pillows in the price of the stay. Some will provide you with bath towels. Some will not allow you to use your own sheets and still require you to rent from them, essentially just automatically raising the rate every person is paying. Some hostels charge for each night of use, while others charge a one-time flat rental rate. Many hostels will do some combination of the above. Most hostels will let you know their requirements on their website or wherever you are booking.

With this in mind, I still chose not to carry my own linens in my backpack. I had a sleeping bag liner for sanitary reasons, but otherwise used what was provided or I paid to rent. This was a trade-off, but it kept me from carrying my own bed linens and having to wash them. However, I took my own lightweight travel towel and only used a towel belonging to the hostel if it was included.

Eating out can get very expensive, so you will probably want to stay in a hostel that has a kitchen/kitchenette. The expansiveness of each cooking area will vary but, at least in my experience, none of the hostels charged for using the kitchen or any of the pots, pans, plates, utensils, etc. Some hostels require an ID or a refundable deposit to make sure you clean the cookware, but if a kitchen is available it is open to everyone.

Lockers are not necessarily guaranteed. Some hostels have stacked metal lockers, while others have rolling baskets that lock underneath the bed. In any case, you will definitely want to bring your own lock. There are almost no hostels that will provide a lock. If you do not have one, you will either have to rent or purchase one from the hostel. Some hostels have lockers for rent that are outside of your room. If possible find a way to lock your items up in the room. For example, you could use a luggage lock to keep the zippers closed and then lock the actual bag to the bed. The bag and your items could still be removed, but it is highly unlikely anyone would go to that much trouble for anything in your bag. Be sure not to show off anything expensive (like a laptop, tablet or camera) and you should be fine with whatever security the hostel provides.

You may want to be strategic and stay in a hostel that has laundry facilities at least every other week, based on your laundry needs. The hostels tend to be cheaper than a laundromat and are certainly much more convenient. You can (and should) wash your clothes in the sink, but occasionally using a machine can get your clothes much cleaner and be very refreshing for your day-to-day experiences. This is not a necessity in every hostel, but something to consider as the days and weeks go by. If you have enough time and at least one complete outfit left, you can pay to just wash your clothes and then air-dry them instead of using a dryer. Again, if you are doing laundry in the hostel it is usually very reasonably priced, but this is just a small way to save a few dollars along the way.

Finally, when staying in hostels, you have to consider who you are traveling with. If you are by yourself and are comfortable in a mixed gender room, this is almost always going to be the best option. If you are not, most hostels have at least one room that is separated by gender. However, it may be a bit more expensive. Also, the more beds in the room, the cheaper it is. If you stay in a 4 person room, you are going to pay a higher price than if you stay in a 10 or 12 person room. Of course, it is a trade-off. The more people, the more likely there is to be noise and other things going on that could make your stay less comfortable. Also, you may wait longer for a bathroom or shower.

In general, the room with the most beds and mixed gender will be the cheapest. It is up to you and what you are willing to do. I traveled with my husband so we always stayed in a mixed room. Many hostels also have private rooms for two people. These are still cheaper than a hotel, but definitely more than any shared room you would find in a hostel. It is up to you what your sleep and comfort are worth while you are backpacking. You can always alternate between room options and still save money, especially when compared to a hotel. If you are exhausted and not sleeping well, consider getting a private room or a 4 bed room for a night or two. You do not want to spend all your money on accommodations, but you definitely want to be healthy and awake to enjoy everything you have planned for your trip.

Another option that is frequently cheaper than hotels is Airbnb. Generally speaking, you will need to reserve these a bit further out. This means you might only want to get an Airbnb occasionally, or only in places that you know you want to interact with more locals. Airbnb is a great way to experience more of the local culture and get a chance to know a local person. They can also be further out of the main tourist part of the city, giving you an opportunity to see something you would have otherwise missed.

Airbnb is also a good way to get a private room for a couple of nights and not have to wait in line for the bathroom. There are usually discounts if you plan to stay a week, so Airbnb might also be a good idea for places that you want to stay longer and settle in for a bit. It is difficult to feel settled in a hostel, but an

Airbnb gives you that opportunity even when you are travelling for an extended amount of time.

Couchsurfing.com is another great way to find a place to sleep. This is completely free! However, much like Airbnb, you may need to make these plans farther out. This is a very popular option because there is no cost. You will just want to be sure you read the reviews and stay with people who are verified in order to be as safe as possible in a situation like this. I personally did not use this option, as most people do not have room for two. However, it is well-liked and it is a great way to get the feel of living as a local in the city you are visiting.

Finally, you have the classic travel options such as a bed and breakfast or a hotel. Both of these are more expensive and will likely not compare to the other options, especially a hostel. However, sometimes it is fun to treat yourself and stay in a nicer room. Depending on how much you are spending eating out, the bed and breakfast might occasionally be worth the cost because it allows you a private room, as well as a home-cooked meal that is usually a classic from the area you are in.

## 5.2 Location, Location, Location

Ultimately, there are a number of options regarding your accommodations while backpacking Europe. It can seem overwhelming, but once you start looking, you will get a feel for what you like and what will best suit your needs and your budget. One other thing to keep in mind is the location. Once you have an idea of what you like, really consider where different accommodations are located.

For instance, you will usually find that the prices of hostels very near to popular tourist destinations are much more expensive than hostels that may be a bit farther away. Taking public transportation will usually not cost more than equivalent of $6-$10 per day, so it is definitely worth taking this into consideration. If the room is $10 or more per day than something farther out, it might not be worth the location. Again, you have to decide how you want to spend your time and what is most important to you. Personally, I would rather spend a small portion of my day using public transportation and save a bit of money for a cup of gelato!

# 5.3 Setting Standards

Finally, when you are finding a place to stay, you need to go in with a few standards. There are some people who are willing to sleep just about anywhere but, generally speaking, you will be happier and healthier if you are getting a good night of sleep. You do not need to be unreasonable in your expectations, because it is just a place to sleep. You are not backpacking Europe to hang out in a hotel. Find a good balance and be sure to read the reviews.

A quick story to illustrate this point: My husband and I were looking for a place to stay in a couple different cities in Poland. We did not realize this at the time, but because Poland is quite a bit cheaper compared to the majority of Europe, many people (Europeans and tourists) go there to party. We were backpacking Europe to actually *see* Europe, including Poland. It turned out that many people were in Poland to drink excessively at a good price. We read the reviews and were happy to see that many were positive, particularly about the location of the hostel. We did not realize that this was because there were many near-by bars. Long story short, if we had read into the reviews a bit more, we would have seen that this hostel was all about parties. That is all fun if you are there to party, but we just ended up exhausted and really not liking the people wandering in loud and drunk at 3am.

It is not always how you want to spend your time, but reading at least a couple pages of reviews will really help you get an idea of if you want to stay somewhere and if the culture of the accommodations fits the kind of trip you are on. We would have happily paid a bit more to be with people that were there to sightsee.

Keep in mind that reviews usually include people who are really upset and people who are blown-away-happy. Try to find a happy medium. This will make your trip more enjoyable, allow you to save money and provide you with the chance to meet new people, both travelers and locals, everywhere you go!

# Chapter 6: Sightseeing

## 6.1 Tourist Attractions

Onto the fun part! During the planning process it can sometimes feel like you have so much work to do and so many options to consider that you are never going to get to see anything. However, all of that prep-work is so that you can enjoy the beautiful sights of Europe and not be overly worried about how expensive some of them can get.

There are so many sights to see in Europe. Even though this is more work you need to do beforehand, it will be the most rewarding time you spend while planning your trip. Consider the route you decided on. It is likely you chose this route because you already have certain things in mind that you want to see. Great! Now you want to go a little deeper and find out what else is in the area. It is a major bummer to find out that you were just a few minutes from something amazing, but you did not know it was there!

Keep in mind that it will be absolutely impossible to see everything. You want to know what is available, but also be content (and maybe overjoyed) that you get to see *anything* in Europe. Many people do not get this chance or know that is even possible to experience Europe on a reasonable budget. So plan, but be flexible and know that some things just will not work out.

One of the great things about many of the iconic European landmarks is that they are free! Figure out what is free in the city you are going to. These are things you will want to see. For example, when in Rome, it will not cost you anything to see the Trevi Fountain or the Spanish Steps. However, keep in mind that these are very old structures and they get a lot of daily traffic. Right before we got to Rome, the Trevi Fountain came out from under scaffolding for the first time in 2 years! On the flipside, the Spanish Steps were fenced off. Again, you cannot see everything. But it is super valuable to make time to go see the free things!

In addition to the free sights, make a list of all the other places you want to visit in each city. You will probably have to narrow this down some, but just start with a big list and work from there. Once you have your list, look up the price of each of these places. Some prices will depend on the time of year, some on your age and some on what kind of admission you want. Ultimately, if you want to see something, see it. This is why you diligently budget in all the other areas. You do not want to miss a once-in-a-lifetime opportunity because you did not budget well for the more mundane parts of your trip.

At this point, you have a couple options. You can really narrow it down to exactly what you want to see, or you can use this list as a guide and choose as you go or based on availability. Some tourist destinations and sights are a bit more difficult to get to or work into your schedule if they require reservations ahead of time. Check out the information and set a general time frame for when you plan to be in each city. Do not throw out ideas you had, as you may find that people you meet would highly recommend something or recently found out a sight is closed. The more you talk with other travelers, the more likely you are to find money-saving tips and general tourist information without doing tons of research. Keep your ears open!

## 6.2 Tours

Reserving a tour is generally a more expensive way to go. Again, you need to prioritize. If there is something you are really interested in and would love to learn all about, take a tour. However, if you just want to see it and move on, you are better off only paying for admission or just wandering around the area if it is free.

An example of this is the Colosseum. When you arrive, there are people outside that want to give you a tour. You can pay them to take you inside and then give you a tour of their own design. In a situation like this, you want to be sure that the business or group is actually going to take you inside the Colosseum and not just take your money and leave. In most places, there is at least an attempt to police this, but certainly no guarantee. Anyway, if you are super interested in the Colosseum, you might want to go this route. However, if you have the basic info you want and just really care to actually see it, you would be better off paying only the price of admission and heading in.

There are almost no tourist destinations and sights that do not provide English signs and tours. You will be able to read pretty much everything. This is a major advantage if you do want to pay for a tour but are definitely still interested in learning about specific things while you are there. Many places also offer audio-tours. These are amazing! They are either included in admission or about €2-€5. If you really want to save money, go with someone and just stand with your heads close together, using the same speaker. You can also take a headphone splitter and each plug in to one system. The audio-tours are always cheaper than a regular tour and you can go at your own pace.

Some places offer tours for free once you have purchased admission. Again, this is just something you will have to research before you go. There are occasionally offers where if you pay for a tour, you can avoid waiting in an entrance line. For example, at the Palace of Versailles, the general admission line to get a ticket and get in can be incredibly long, sometimes an hour or more. Buying your ticket online does not guarantee faster entrance, as there are still security lines and this is a destination that is incredibly popular with tour buses. So, you can purchase a ticket for a tour online (along with your admission ticket), go in a side entrance, take an hour long tour, and then be in the palace. At that point, you can explore all the areas open to the general public, plus you got to tour a part that not everyone gets to see.

Each place that you want to see will probably have some little tip or trick to either save you money or time. While this is mainly about budgeting your money, it is so important to remember that your time is worth something, as well.

One option that is always interesting and fun is to go on a free walking tour. These are run by different companies and the way it works is slightly different for each tour guide, but for the tourist it is always the same: free! Of course, the polite thing to do is a leave a tip to thank them for their time. This is a great way to start out your visit in a city. You can get a feel for the area and get some good information from other people who have been there longer. You can even talk with the tour guide. It is an inexpensive but interesting overview of the place you are visiting.

If you do choose to take a free walking tour, please tip. Yes, the tour guides enjoy what they do but they are also still trying to earn money. A good tip is anywhere from $10-$20 per person. This might seem like a lot at first, but if you were to take a tour that you were required to schedule, you would end up paying quite a bit more. Also, many guides will give you an idea of what people tip. Use your best judgment.

There are some places that you will want to see that are going to be difficult to reach on your own. For example, Stonehenge is not exactly on the way to anything in London. This is a situation where you will want to just pay the money for a half-day or full-day tour. When something like this comes up, do not be discouraged and choose to skip this. You will regret not seeing something just because it cost you more than your average day.

Because you are hopefully doing research ahead of time, these things should not come as a surprise to you. Once you know when you will be in a city, start looking for tours that are available. You do not necessarily need the nicest or most expensive tour, but you will want to find a tour that will get you to your destination(s) and include your cost of admission.

We did not do very many tours like this, but we did choose to utilize this option for a couple different sights. One tour included Bath, Stonehenge and Windsor Castle. That one was out of London and was a full day. Another we did was a full day in Northern Island, with the Giant's Causeway being the main attraction. You will need to decide if there is a reasonable way to get to certain places or if it would be better to just pay for a tour. It really depends on what you want to see and where you are staying.

Bike tours are another good way to hear from a local and see quite a few sights at once, usually at a pretty good price. Bike tours also allow you more opportunities to speak with the guide, since they have to be a smaller group.

There are a number of other types of tours you can go on, but it will depend on if you are interested in what is being offered and if the tour will provide you with something that you could otherwise experience on your own. Again, do your research and you will be able to make a wise financial decision, as well as see the majority of what you are interested in.

# 6.3 Discounts

Discounts are pretty widely available for a lot of major tourist destinations in the big cities, but you do have to look for them. One of the great options in a lot of cities is a city pass, or something similar. This is a one-time purchase that grants you admission to a set list of sights. To decide if a city-wide pass is right for you, figure out if you will go to enough places on the pass to equal the amount you would separately spend on admission. Even if you end up not getting a city pass, it is a great way to find out about some of the more obscure things in the area.

If you get a city pass, there are often additional discounts included. These can range from a percentage off at a restaurant to half off on a souvenir. There are occasionally coupons like this also included in regular admission to certain sights. Always check the bulletins and pamphlets in the place you are staying, along with at the ticket desk of the tourist sights.

Many of the major attractions in Europe offer free or discounted days once a week or once a month. Some even offer discounted evening rates. You can find this information online. If you can plan your stay around a free admission day, that is great! However, be prepared to wait in longer lines and experience generally larger crowds. Many people like to take advantage of free things!

If you are under 25 years old or are a student, you qualify for lots of discounts. The best way to get these discounts is to get an International Student ID card (ISIC) while you are actually still a student at a college or university. You can order these online or go to a local office. These are proof that you are a student and will allow you to qualify for discounted admission rates and occasionally even discounted food. You do have to pay a one-time fee to get the card, but the savings will definitely outweigh the upfront cost. You can try to get discounts based on just your age, but the card is recognized all over the world and is the best way to go.

In general, discounts are available but you do to have search for them. Sometimes the place you are staying will have a deal with a nearby restaurant that will give you a discount. If you go to the travel center or tourist information desk in the city, you will likely find some available discounts. However, the most consistent and best way to get discounts is to travel while you are a student or shortly after graduating. If you can, take advantage of that time you have and your sense of adventure while you are young – it will pay off.

# Chapter 7: Eating

## 7.1 Restaurants

Eating meals all over Europe is something that gets a lot of people excited. Who doesn't love some good food?! Unfortunately, this also means that a budget can get out of control when it comes to eating. If you eat out at a restaurant every single day, at least two meals a day, you will likely go way over budget.

This is surprising to a lot of people, but most restaurants charge for water. So even ordering water (which would save you money in the States) can quickly add up. For this reason, you should pack a water bottle, as mentioned in the packing list. I filled my water bottle up from the tap of wherever we were staying every single morning and never had a problem. It is just a generally good idea to drink water, but you will especially be glad to save that money. Of course, it is okay to splurge and get something else to drink, but counting on having your own water is always a good idea.

Again, just like when you are at home, eating out for most meals is not a good way to save money. Of course, you should experience the local cuisine as much as you are interested. However, it is safe to say that not all locals go to a nice sit-down restaurant for dinner every night. So, to save money and stick with your budget, you will need to get a little creative. Consider sharing meals if you go out with someone.

You could also order two dishes you both want to try and then each eat half. This gives you a wide range and a chance to try more food without having to eat out most meals.

The rules for tipping vary in each city, so you will absolutely want to look this up before you go somewhere. You are likely used to just automatically tipping at home, but tipping is definitely not expected everywhere you go. If you are tipping and it is unnecessary, you are using money you could be spending somewhere else. However, you also want to be polite and follow the customs of whatever culture you are visiting. Look this up each time you arrive in a new city so that you can confidently close out a bill at a restaurant.

One thing to note is that if a restaurant is located really close to a major tourist destination, the prices are probably marked up and you are not necessarily getting a classic meal from that culture. Instead, you are getting the Americanized version of something at a ridiculous price. If possible, walk at least two to three blocks away from the popular sight and then start looking for food. Also, if the menu has pictures, that restaurant is catering to tourists. It does tend to make ordering easier, but you are not saving money and you are likely not getting a true local meal.

Eat out at restaurants when you really want to, but do not make this your main source of food. You will quickly overspend and, consequently, miss out on other things you could have used that money for.

## 7.2 Fast Food

Eating the local version of fast food in each city is a good way to experience some different dishes without the expense of a formal sit-down meal. It is also nice because during the day you may not have a lot of time to sit down between sightseeing and tours, but that does not mean you will not want to eat. Try to find some places that the locals go to grab a bite during their lunch break. The staff at your hostel or hotel is a great resource for discovering a place like this. Also, if you are brave, stop someone on the street and ask them for a recommendation in the area. I cannot guarantee everyone will be polite, but in my experience people were usually happy to give a quick suggestion for a meal. Food unites people. Take advantage of this. It will get you a good meal and help you save some money.

You also have the option of eating at fast food chains that you recognize from the States. There is no shortage of McDonald's, Pizza Hut, Subway, etc. While I would not recommend that you make this kind of fast food your go-to, sometimes it is the easiest and fastest option when you are rushing around and trying to see everything. The prices are usually comparable to US prices, so not awful. However, you could also get fast food from a local chain for a comparable price. Use this option sparingly.

## 7.3 Local Supermarkets

Shopping in local supermarkets and preparing your own food is the most cost-effective way to go. While this does not sound exotic and exciting, it is actually a great option and still gives you a feel for the local culture. Every country will have different items stocking the shelves of the supermarket. You can learn a lot about what people eat when they get off of a long day of work and just grab something from their fridge at home.

Many cultures eat bread and cheese as a meal. This really can sustain you for lunch, or serve as a light dinner. If you are staying in a hostel, you can actually cook a meal. If you do not want to try new things in a hostel, pasta and sauce are always an option. You can also get your own breakfast items (like milk and cereal) if you are going to be somewhere for a few days.

The supermarkets are a great way to learn about the local culture and get an idea of what the locals are eating. They are also huge money-savers. You will spend a fraction of the money on a supermarket meal compared to what you would spend going out.

## 7.4 Drinks

Drinking alcohol in Europe is a very different experience compared to drinking alcohol in the States. However, it is not necessarily any cheaper. There are certain places that a glass of wine will seem unbelievably cheap (like Italy or Portugal) but, generally speaking, purchasing alcohol one glass or pint at a time will still add up quickly. If you are not backpacking for the sake of partying, you will be better off limiting how much alcohol you purchase. Again, it is about priorities. If you spend the equivalent of 30 USD a week on alcohol, that is another night you could stay or one admission ticket. It is just something to keep in mind while traveling. It is definitely worth trying something new and experiencing the local culture, but you will want to purchase alcohol in moderation.

# Chapter 8: Extra spending

## 8.1 Surprises

As with all of life, there will be surprises along the way that will cost you money. You will want to make sure you have a little bit of money available for these, as mentioned in the original budgeting chapter. Things will happen and you will have to spend money that you were not necessarily counting on. Try to be prepared for these things, otherwise it could be a stressful situation made worse by the state of your budget.

Of course, some surprises can be good, like you discovered the ultimate tour that you absolutely cannot miss. Or you could come across a restaurant that you have seen on TV and absolutely must eat at. Then, you can feel okay spending the money because you had it budgeted. Just like with everyday life, the main thing is to be financially prepared to handle the unexpected.

## 8.2 Souvenirs

Depending on the type of person you are, you may need to budget quite a bit for souvenirs or you may not need to write in much at all. This is completely arbitrary and up to you. Personally, I am not a big souvenir person. I bought a pair of Birkenstocks in Germany (because how could I not?). Other than this, I bought one book. In four months of travel and 17 countries, those are the only souvenirs I came home with. Therefore, a budget of about 150 USD was plenty for me.

However, if you love souvenirs and you like to buy gifts for you friends and family, you will need a bigger budget. If you are carrying only a backpack, you will not have the space for many souvenirs. This also means you will need to ship them home. This can get expensive. Souvenirs are definitely a personal decision, but you should consider what your plan is before you leave the house, as this can become a place in your budget that quickly goes negative.

# 8.3 Emergencies

While it is impossible to foresee any potential emergencies, it is really helpful to have a plan in case something goes wrong. Even if you do not have the cash available for a major emergency, consider a plan and how you would handle it. Either make sure you have enough credit or have a way to receive money from someone back in the States. Hopefully nothing drastic happens, but it is good to have the peace of mind so you can enjoy your trip to the fullest.

# Conclusion

Here are some final tips that aren't related to your budget, but that will make your trip even more exciting: Keep a travel journal. It can be hard work and sometimes you might not want to, but after it's all said and done, you will be glad you did. Even if you just write down where you want and one cool memory, it's worth it.

Almost every city has a tower or a church or something that will allow you to go up very high and look down over everything. Take advantage of this! No two cities look the same and this is a super cool way to get your bearings. Just be prepared to climb a lot of stairs.

Eat gelato as much as possible! You will never get to eat gelato as good as what's available in Italy. Seriously.

Consider going without cell service. You will save money and smart phones have maps that will track you, even without service. Most hostels have free Wi-Fi, so use that to prepare and then grab a map and go for it! You may get a little lost, but it will be super rewarding to travel without relying on your phone or being attached to your phone the whole time you're there.

Take lots of pictures! But also remember that the internet probably already has a way better picture than the one you're going to take (and probably there won't be crowds in the internet pictures), so be sure to actually get pictures with you in them. Spend a couple minutes getting these. Then move on and look at the sight uninhibited by a screen.

Backpacking on a budget is so rewarding. There is a lot of work that goes into it upfront, but the benefits are huge. If you are willing to spend a little less on the creature comforts, you will have the opportunity to see many sights and experience many cultures in a way that you will likely never get to again. Many people think that going on an extended trip to Europe is lucky, but if you do it, you will know that it was hard work, saving and planning that allowed you to enjoy Europe in such a unique way.

Go before this kind of travel is not appealing to you or you cannot get this much time off work. Experience all the sights you want to see, meet new people, try new food and makes lots of memories. You will have a trip that is just as fulfilling as the person who spent $10,000 in one week, instead of over the course of months.

I wrote this for a blogpost the last week of my trip and it perfectly sums up my excitement and why you should not let the dream to backpack Europe pass you by, no matter your current situation: "Go. Now. Before it's too late. If you want to go, make it a priority. Don't be like the people that finally get here and are too old to walk halfway down the Eiffel Tower or ride their bike around the Irish coast. Don't miss out on the chance to sunbathe topless in Barcelona or run through a train station like a mad person. Don't risk waiting until your body won't allow for a 4-course Italian meal or a full day of not eating. You don't want to get here and be the people that have only 1 hour to enjoy the most beautiful scenery on earth and 20 hours to travel home. Don't wait until the dream trip just presents itself... Luck will not get you here. Hard work and planning are necessary. We wouldn't be here if we had let the fear of unemployment, no savings and no place to call our own win over the desire to go and do."

Go backpack Europe (on a budget).

# About the Expert

Kacey Andreacola graduated from the University of Arizona with an English degree after getting married the previous weekend. She and her husband then spent 4 months backpacking Europe as the first step in fulfilling their dream of adventure. They loosely planned out their trip but made plenty of adjustments as they learned along the way.

Kacey and her husband moved from Tucson, AZ to Seattle, WA where she now writes, edits and works at a non-profit that ships medical supplies overseas. She loves reading, blogging (sundaycereal.wordpress.com), drinking coffee, planning new adventures and enjoying the natural beauty all around her.

HowExpert publishes quick 'how to' guides on all topics from A to Z by everyday experts. Visit HowExpert.com to learn more.

# Recommended Resources

- HowExpert.com – Quick 'How To' Guides on All Topics from A to Z by Everyday Experts.
- HowExpert.com/free – Free HowExpert Email Newsletter.
- HowExpert.com/books – HowExpert Books
- HowExpert.com/courses – HowExpert Courses
- HowExpert.com/membership – HowExpert Membership Site
- HowExpert.com/writers – Write About Your #1 Passion/Knowledge/Expertise & Become a HowExpert Author.
- HowExpert.com/resources – Additional HowExpert Recommended Resources
- YouTube.com/HowExpert – Subscribe to HowExpert YouTube.
- Instagram.com/HowExpert – Follow HowExpert on Instagram.
- Facebook.com/HowExpert – Follow HowExpert on Facebook.

Made in United States
Troutdale, OR
12/14/2024